HOLLYWOOD
KIDS

EDITED BY J. C. SUARÈS
TEXT BY J. SPENCER BECK

THOMASSON-GRANT

Published by Thomasson-Grant, Inc.

Copyright © 1994 J. C. Suarès.
Captions copyright © 1994 J. Spencer Beck.

Printed in Hong Kong.

ISBN 1-56566-067-6

00 99 98 97 96 95 94 5 4 3 2 1

Inquiries should be directed to:
Thomasson-Grant, Inc.
One Morton Drive, Suite 500
Charlottesville, VA 22903-6806
(804) 977-1780

Jackie Cooper, Mickey Rooney,
and Freddie Bartholomew, 1936

*Poised poolside at the Hollywood home of W. S. Van Dyke,
director of their upcoming film,* The Devil Is a Sissy, *the three veteran
actors (all of whom had faced the cameras before their third birthdays)
had already become top box-office stars by the beginning of the 1930s.
The rather banal story of the sweet child (Bartholomew) of divorcing
parents who takes up with two toughs from the wrong side of the tracks,
Van Dyke's film drew crowds, thanks to the electricity generated by the
triple-treat star power of the MGM production's ensemble cast.*

from the two Jackies (Cooper and Coogan), to Shirley Temple, Mickey Rooney, and Macaulay Culkin, some of Hollywood's smallest stars have managed to outshine some of its biggest in movies that have become classics for all time. Decade after decade, for nearly a century, tiny tots have managed to steal the best scenes (and moviegoers' hearts) and become big-box-office babes overnight.

Although she was already in her teens when she first faced the cameras, immortal screen queen and movie mogul Mary Pickford started the game playing adorable child-women half her age. When she finally cut her legendary golden locks (at 35 years of age!), the stage was set for actual toddlers like Jackie *"The Kid"* Coogan and the original Little Rascals to charm silent-era audiences with their mischievous pranks and wide-eyed innocence.

It took the precocious song-and-dance talents (not to mention the dimpled cheeks) of a bank teller's daughter from Santa Monica, California, however, to make the men in the front office really sit up and take notice. The quintessential child star, little curly Shirley Temple charmed the pants off of Depression-weary audiences (and emptied their pants pockets in the process!). Churning out as many as nine films a year, the diminutive dynamo was the first juvenile actor to receive an Oscar and paved the way for every child star who followed in her tiny footsteps.

Not everyone was as talented (or lucky) as Temple, of course, and thousands of stage-struck children of star-struck stage moms had the studio doors slammed in their faces after a picture or two. Overnight sensations like Claude Jarman, Jr., and Peggy Ann Garner may have won Oscars their first time at bat, but their big-league debuts didn't translate into long-lived success, and both their careers languished after only a few pictures.

It has always been next to impossible for young stars to make the transition from adorable child roles to more mature parts, and the few who have succeeded can be counted on the fingers of one hand. Arguably a better actress as a youngster, little Natasha Gurdin blossomed into a fetching leading lady as Natalie Wood, and Elizabeth Taylor has never stopped wowing (or shocking) us since her starring debut half a century ago with a horse named Pie.

In more recent times, pint-size phenomena from Patty Duke and Mary Badham to Brooke Shields and Drew Barrymore have struggled to bridge the gap from child star to adult headliner—with varying degrees of success. Only super-smart Jodie Foster has managed to segue from precocious child actress to Oscar winner (and director!) with seeming ease.

No book on Hollywood kids would be complete without mentioning the latest small-fry to take on Tinseltown. Becoming the richest child actor in movie history following his seven-figure deal to appear in the follow-up of the box-office bonanza, *Home Alone*, Macaulay Culkin has gone on to become a mini movie mogul to be reckoned with (and the powers-that-be in Hollywood are listening). Mary Pickford would be proud.

Jackie Coogan (with Jack Coogan Sr. and Patricia Marks), 1921 (above)

Jackie Coogan (with Charlie Chaplin)
THE KID, 1921 (RIGHT)

The son of vaudeville entertainers, the bright-eyed six-year-old with the famous rumpled bob became an overnight sensation when Chaplin cast him as his costar in the box-office silent smash The Kid. *Soon one of the richest actors in Hollywood (his contract with Metro would earn him $1 million per year), the mini movie mogul was beset by money problems later in his career, when his parents refused to part with their son's earnings. Inspiring the passage of The Coogan Bill, which protected child actors from such abuses in the future, Hollywood's original child star resurfaced many years later as a bit actor in mostly "B" films and as the gruesome Uncle Fester in "The Addams Family" TV show.*

Jackie Cooper and Jackie Coogan, 1928

*Although both actors had started in films not long after they
could walk, Coogan was already a veteran star when this backlot
publicity shot was taken during Hollywood's silent-era heyday. About to
become a star in his own right thanks to his role in fifteen of the original
"Our Gang" two-reelers, Cooper would make a bigger mark later
in the 1930s, in films such as* The Champ, Dinky, *and a
remake of buddy Coogan's 1921 hit,* Peck's Bad Boy.

Scotty Beckett and George "Spanky" McFarland, 1934 (above)

Billie "Buckwheat" Thomas, Darla "Cookie" Hood, George "Spanky" McFarland, Carl "Alfalfa" Switzer, and Edith Fellows (with Bing Crosby), 1935 (right)

With an ever-changing cast that helped to reinvigorate the long-running comedy series (renamed "The Little Rascals" for television in 1955), the "Our Gang" shorts reached the apex of their popularity in 1936, when Bored of Education *won an Academy Award for Best Short Film. Inspired by the tremendous public interest in Jackie Coogan after his 1921 performance in* The Kid, *producer Hal Roach went on to make 221 mini-features over the next twenty years, making household names of beloved characters such as "Farina," "Spanky," and "Alfalfa" (the latter here in a publicity shot for his "Our Gang" debut,* Our Gang Follies of 1936).

Our Gang (The Little Rascals), 1928

*Posing innocently with their "teacher" for a publicity pic
for their upcoming two-reel short,* School Begins, *tiny troublemakers
Harry Spear, Joe Cobb, Bobby "Wheezer" Hutchins, Jean Darling,
Mary Ann Jackson, and Allen "Farina" Hoskins (along with Pete the
Pup) were the second group of kids to be incarnated for the "Our Gang"
shorts begun six years earlier. When the popular series went from silent
to sound with episode number 89 the following year, the pint-size
players had a bit of trouble remembering their lines (not to mention
calling each other by their characters' nicknames for the first time).
They were soon joined by pouty-lipped charmer Jackie Cooper,
who led the pack into the "talkie" era.*

Shirley Temple

THE LITTLE COLONEL, 1935

Although she had already won a special Oscar in 1934,
Hollywood's most celebrated child star would make her best pictures
in the following few years, including this lavishly produced Twentieth
Century-Fox film about a steely little magnolia who single-handedly ends
a family feud in the post-Civil War South. With a preternatural matu-
rity that belied her innocent on-screen persona, the six-year-old future
United States ambassador to Ghana and Czechoslovakia once remarked:
"I stopped believing in Santa Claus when Mother took me to see him
in a department store and he asked for my autograph."

Shirley Temple (with Frank Morgan, left), 1936
*Between takes on a set that was meant to simulate
New York City's Central Park in 1850, the seven-year-
old seasoned pro discusses an upcoming scene with the
director (William Seiter) of the box-office hit* Dimples.
*A typically heartwarming story about a little girl who
helps win her Bowery-bum grandpa (Morgan)
a place in the hearts of high society, the film (the star's
twentieth in four years!) marked a midpoint in the
hardworking actress's big-box-office run.*

Shirley Temple (with Buddy Ebsen)

CAPTAIN JANUARY, 1936

*Costarring old-timers Guy Kibbee, Slim Summerville,
and Hollywoods's favorite song-and-dance "hillbilly," Buddy Ebsen, this
standard-fare curly Shirley story about a little girl who is rescued from a
shipwreck by a lighthouse keeper still managed to pack in audiences, who
never seemed to get enough of Twentieth Century-Fox's biggest box-
office attraction. Appropriately named "Star" this time out, Temple
lived up to the cheesy moniker, singing and dancing with Ebsen in
one of her legendary musical routines, "At the Codfish Ball."*

Mickey Rooney (with Morgan Farley)

BELOVED, 1934

*Having become an indispensable part of his family's vaudeville
act at 15 months of age, the child star who never grew up first made his
mark on screen in the late silent and early sound era in some 50 two-reel
comedies as the comic-strip-like title character in the "Mickey McGuire"
series. Born Joe Yule, Jr., in Brooklyn, New York, the future star of the
popular "Andy Hardy" series and the most-married man in Hollywood
began getting small film roles as "Mickey Rooney" by the early 1930s,
including a bit part as a future concert virtuoso in this small-
budget biopic from Universal Studios.*

Mickey Rooney

A MIDSUMMER NIGHT'S DREAM, 1935

*A daring venture for Warner Bros., a studio known for its
"working-class" melodramas, this eagerly awaited film adaptation
of one of the Bard's best-loved plays won an Oscar for its sumptuous
photography and made a bona fide star of the fourteen-year-old Rooney.
Even with a cleverly concealed broken leg (the result of a tobogganing
accident during a mid-production break), the appealing adolescent
garnered critical kudos as a memorably faerie-like Puck and went
on four years later to unseat fellow child sensation Shirley Temple
as Hollywood's number-one box-office star.*

Jackie Cooper (with Wallace Beery, above)
THE CHAMP, 1931 (ABOVE)
DINKY, 1935 (RIGHT)

Nominated for an Academy Award in 1930 for his teary-eyed performance in Skippy *(to induce tears, the star was told his dog would be shot!), America's favorite "little tough guy" cried up a storm the following year as the adoring son of washed-up prizefighter Beery in King Vidor's* The Champ. *Failing to successfully make the transition from his child-star leads in films such as* Dinky, The Bowery, *and* Treasure Island *to more adult roles, Cooper re-emerged many years later as a powerful television executive and made some well-publicized cameo appearances in the Superman films of the 1980s.*

Freddie Bartholomew (with W. C. Fields)

DAVID COPPERFIELD, 1935

Unable, like many child stars, to make the transition to adult roles (he later became an advertising executive), the British-born actor with the angelic face and perfect diction will forever be remembered for the boy-hero roles he played in celebrated Hollywood versions of adventure classics such as Captains Courageous, Kidnapped, *and* The Swiss Family Robinson. *Garnering overnight stardom in the highly acclaimed George Cukor-directed* David Copperfield *(his first American film), Bartholomew made his title-role turn in* Little Lord Fauntleroy *the following year one of the most memorable parts in child-star history.*

Freddie Bartholomew (with Greta Garbo)

ANNA KARENINA, 1935

*Despite a humble British background, the ten-year-old veteran actor
(he had started on the London stage at three) possessed a mild-mannered
refinement that made him a natural to play Sergei, the mother-sick son
of the tragic heroine in this classic MGM version of Leo Tolstoy's famous
novel. The perfect little gentleman no matter what film he appeared in,
Bartholomew's saccharine-sweet type fell out of favor by the end
of WWII, and the star's career languished as a result.*

Freddie Bartholomew (with Spencer Tracy)
CAPTAINS COURAGEOUS, 1937

Although his "proper" screen persona was perfect for his role as a spoiled rich kid who learns about life from fisherman Tracy (who won his first Oscar for the part), Bartholomew suffered an off-screen life in 1937 that was anything but. Having relinquished custody of their child years before to an aunt who reared him, the actor's parents resurfaced to get him back at the height of the thirteen-year-old's popularity (and earning power) at the same time that the aunt was attempting to free him from his MGM contract (both efforts failed). With his film career all but over within the decade, Bartholomew eventually moved to television and then to advertising before his death in 1992 at the age of 68.

951-

Judy Garland, 1939

Posing for a pre-release publicity picture on the set of
The Wizard of Oz *with the film's director, Victor Fleming,*
producer, Mervyn LeRoy, and a passel of Munchkinland's
diminutive denizens, the "little girl with the great big voice"
born Frances Gumm won a special Oscar for the role that was
originally offered to past Oscar-winner and fellow child star
Shirley Temple. An overnight legend thanks to her endearing
performance as the wide-eyed girl from Kansas, the real-life star
suffered from a sadistic stage mom ("She was the real Wicked
Witch of the West," the actress once remarked), drug addiction,
and chronic depression. Despite enormous success as an actress and,
later, concert-hall singer, the performer died of an overdose of
sleeping pills soon after her forty-seventh birthday.

33

Margaret O'Brien and Judy Garland

MEET ME IN ST. LOUIS, 1944

Never lovelier (thanks largely to a studio-prescribed regimen of diet pills
and the makeover talents of Carole Lombard's former beauty guru,
Dottie Pondell), the twenty-one-year-old superstar was paired with the
six-year-old newcomer for this Oscar-winning Vincente Minnelli-directed
musical. Although O'Brien (who won a special Oscar in 1944) never
successfully made the transition to more mature roles, Garland, who took
Minnelli as the second of her eventual five husbands, would go on to star
in a number of important musicals throughout the 1940s and 1950s.

Baby LeRoy (with Mischa Auer and W. C. Fields), 1933

The itsy-bitsy bugbear of baby-baiting W. C. Fields (who once spiked the infant's milk with gin!), Tinseltown's most famous tot appeared in four of the celebrated curmudgeon's celluloid farces before he could even walk. Following in the tiny footsteps of silent-era toddlers Baby Parsons and Baby Peggy, little LeRoy Winebrenner was given a seven-year contract (signed when he was eight months old!) but retired from the screen at the ripe age of four.

Gabriel Dell, Bobby Jordan, Leo Gorcey, Billy Halop,
Bernard Punsley, and Huntz Hall

DEAD END, 1937

Reprising the roles they had played in the Broadway hit by
Sidney Kingsley, the Dead End Kids became overnight movie stars as
the New York City toughs who learn about life the hard way in this
critically acclaimed Samuel Goldwyn film adaptation starring Humphrey
Bogart. Making a tremendous impact on young movie audiences, the
silver screen's most celebrated street kids went on to make an incredible
86 films (with occasional cast changes) as The Dead End Kids and
Little Tough Guys, The East Side Kids, and, finally, as the aging
delinquents in Monogram Pictures' big-box-office Bowery Boys
comedies of the 1940s and 1950s.

Natalie Wood (with Orson Welles), 1945 (above)

Natalie Wood (with Edmund Gwenn)

MIRACLE ON 34TH STREET, 1947 (RIGHT)

*Although the petite blonde-haired, blue-eyed daughter of a
Russian architect and ballet dancer of French extraction became a bona
fide child star as the Santa-scoffing Susan Walker in the Christmas
classic* Miracle on 34th Street, *the six-year-old Natasha Gurdin
managed to steal a few scenes from veteran actor Orson Welles in*
Tomorrow Is Forever, *her second film. One of the few child actors who
made the difficult transition to adult lead, the late star racked up three
Oscar nominations in later years despite the ignominy of being
commemorated annually by the Harvard Lampoon's
"Natalie Wood Award" for worst performances by an actress.*

Peggy Ann Garner and Ted Donaldson (with Joan Blondell)
A TREE GROWS IN BROOKLYN, 1945
*This much-loved sentimental saga of a young girl's budding hope
amid the poverty of turn-of-the-century Williamsburg, Brooklyn, earned
thirteen-year-old Garner (who had begun modeling when she was five)
a Best Child Actor Oscar and put Donaldson on the movie map for the
first time. A classic case study of most child stars' short-term celluloid
longevity, Donaldson's career was over almost as soon as it began, while
Garner's languished until the end of the decade. Garner tried her hand
at Broadway in the 1950s before surfacing as a real-estate broker
and then sales manager for a California auto dealership prior
to her early death in 1984 at the age of 53.*

Roddy McDowall
LASSIE, COME HOME, 1943 (ABOVE)
Elizabeth Taylor
NATIONAL VELVET, 1944 (RIGHT)

Two of the most popular child actors of the 1940s made their
mark upstaging their four-legged costars in these sentimental family
favorites from MGM. Although the violet-eyed future love goddess
appeared with fellow Brit-born McDowall in the first of the Lassie
movies, Taylor's preternatural poise and adult-like beauty made her an
overnight sensation the following year in the most celebrated horse-racing
saga of all time. Taylor and McDowall continued as film stars (and
close friends) throughout the ensuing decades and remain two
of the few MGM-processed child stars to have survived
the big-studio days relatively unscathed.

John Howard Davies

OLIVER TWIST, 1948

Called by Time *magazine "no less a classic than the Dickens
novel which it brings to life," this magnificently staged and poignantly
acted version of the much-filmed Victorian tearjerker made the sweet-
faced eight-year-old lead player a star his first time out. Although
he would make only two more screen appearances, the British-born
son of screenwriter Jack Davies found great success years later as
the BBC television director who helmed the popular "Monty
Python's Flying Circus" comedy series, among others.*

Brandon de Wilde
SHANE, 1953 (ABOVE)

*As talented an actor as any adult film star, the Brooklyn-born
son of a stage-manager father and actress mother made an auspicious
debut at the age of seven in 492 performances of the Broadway hit*
The Member of the Wedding. *The first juvenile ever to win the
theater world's coveted Donaldson Award, de Wilde starred in the film
version of the play the following year, before garnering international
acclaim as the Shane-adoring Wyoming youngster in George Stevens's
Western classic. Later starring in his own TV series ("Jamie") and
in well-received films such as* All Fall Down *and* Hud, *de Wilde
died tragically in a traffic accident at the age of 30.*

Claude Jarman, Jr. (with Gregory Peck)
THE YEARLING, 1946 (RIGHT)

*Having won a special Oscar his first time out for his sensitive
portrayal of the lonely, deer-loving only child of a hard-strapped back-
woods couple, the eleven-year-old Hollywood greenhorn wowed audiences
again three years later in* Intruder in the Dust. *Quickly fading into
obscurity afterwards, Jarman re-emerged successfully over two decades
later as the executive producer of the rock-concert feature film*
Fillmore *and as the manager of the San Francisco Opera House.*

Mary Badham (with Gregory Peck)
TO KILL A MOCKINGBIRD, 1962

The film that finally earned Peck an Academy Award for
Best Actor (after five previous nominations) also garnered the nine-
year-old newcomer who played his winsome daughter a nomination for
Best Supporting Actress. Losing to another child actress, Patty Duke,
who gave an outstanding performance that year as Helen Keller in
The Miracle Worker, *Badham had even more trouble than Duke*
sustaining her film career, and made just two more pictures
before retiring from the screen in her mid-teens.

George Winslow (with Marilyn Monroe)

GENTLEMEN PREFER BLONDES, 1953

With fewer movies being made after the death of the studio system by the 1950s, many child actors found it easier to maintain careers on television than on the big screen. Nevertheless, film actors such as Brandon de Wilde, Billy Chapin, "Bad Seed" Patty McCormack, Kevin "Moochie" Corcoran, and George "Foghorn" Winslow enjoyed some measure of success throughout the decade. More famous for his bullfrog-throated basso than his acting talents, Winslow appeared in a number of movies, including this legendary Marilyn Monroe-Jane Russell comedy, before retiring his "little-boy-with-a-big-voice" gimmick forever at the age of twelve.

Patty Duke (with Anne Bancroft)
THE MIRACLE WORKER, 1962

*Long before she had become one of television's best-loved
juvenile stars, the pint-size actress born into a broken home in Queens,
New York, had two films, some fifty TV appearances, and numerous
stage performances behind her before rocketing to stardom as the thirteen-
year-old lead in the Broadway smash about the life of Helen Keller.
Reprising her role for the film version three years later, Duke became
the youngest Best Supporting Actress winner in Hollywood history, but
went on to find more success in TV dramas than on the big-screen
after "The Patty Duke Show" ended its run in 1965.*

Linda Blair (with Richard Burton)

EXORCIST II: THE HERETIC, 1977

*Despite special effects such as the thousands of British locusts
imported to California for this particularly harrowing scene, the first of
two sequels of the controversial 1973 chiller by director William Friedkin
was a box-office bomb that failed to reignite the career of its equally
controversial juvenile lead. Nominated for a Best Supporting Actress
Oscar for that original effort, the Westport, Connecticut-born actress
continues to be plagued by her demonic typecasting in low-budget
shockers such as* Savage Island, Grotesque, The Chilling,
Repossessed, *and* The Fatal Bond.

Justin Henry (with Dustin Hoffman)
KRAMER VS. KRAMER, 1979 (ABOVE)

*Stealing most of the scenes from veterans Hoffman and Meryl Streep in this pastel-colored update of the classic three-hanky Hollywood soaper, the seven-year-old towheaded newcomer went up against former child star and Oscar-winner Mickey Rooney (*The Black Stallion*) in the Best Supporting Actor category (both lost to Melvyn Douglas in* Being There*). Exhibiting the same sweet-faced naturalness in front of the camera that has spelled success for most great child performers (and which rarely translates to success in more mature parts), Henry has since segued into roles in teenybopper fare such as* Sixteen Candles *and* Sweet Hearts Dance*—with moderate success.*

Mara Hobel (with Faye Dunaway)
MOMMIE DEAREST, 1981 (RIGHT)

Although it didn't make her a star, the unknown nine-year-old will forever be remembered for her convincingly chilling performance as the spectacularly abused daughter of Hollywood's durable glamour queen and adoptive-mother-from-Hell, Joan Crawford. No easy task playing against the indomitable Dunaway herself, Hobel holds her own against the veteran Oscar-winner, whose larger-than-life, wire-hanger-wielding star turn helped make the picture an instant camp classic.

Tatum O'Neal (with Ryan O'Neal)
PAPER MOON, 1973

The daughter of Ryan and future wife of tennis ace John McEnroe broke Patty Duke's record as the youngest performer ever to win a Best Supporting Actress Oscar for her film debut as the nine-year-old tough-talking, chain-smoking con artist in this Depression-era comedy from director Peter Bogdanovich. Although her follow-up three years later in the big-box-office Bad News Bears *made O'Neal the highest-paid child star in movie history ($350,000 plus 9 percent of the film's considerable profits), the abrasive actress seriously damaged her career with subsequent schlockers such as* Nickelodeon, Little Darlings, *and* International Velvet, *a sacrilegious remake of the 1944 Elizabeth Taylor original.*

Jodie Foster and Scott Baio, above

BUGSY MALONE, 1976 (ABOVE)

TAXI DRIVER, 1976 (RIGHT)

Along with Elizabeth Taylor and Natalie Wood, Foster is one of the few child stars who successfully bridged the gap between juvenile and adult roles. Cast in a number of Disney TV productions in the 1960s, the mature-beyond-her-years twelve-year-old future Yale graduate shocked audiences with her uncanny portrayals of a pre-teen prostitute and a gangster's moll in these two back-to-back Oscar contenders. Although Foster would surpass her fourteen-year-old Bugsy Malone *costar (he played the title role) and go on to become one of America's most sought-after film actresses, Baio followed up his auspicious big-screen debut with phenomenal success on the small screen, in TV series such as "Happy Days" and "Charles in Charge."*

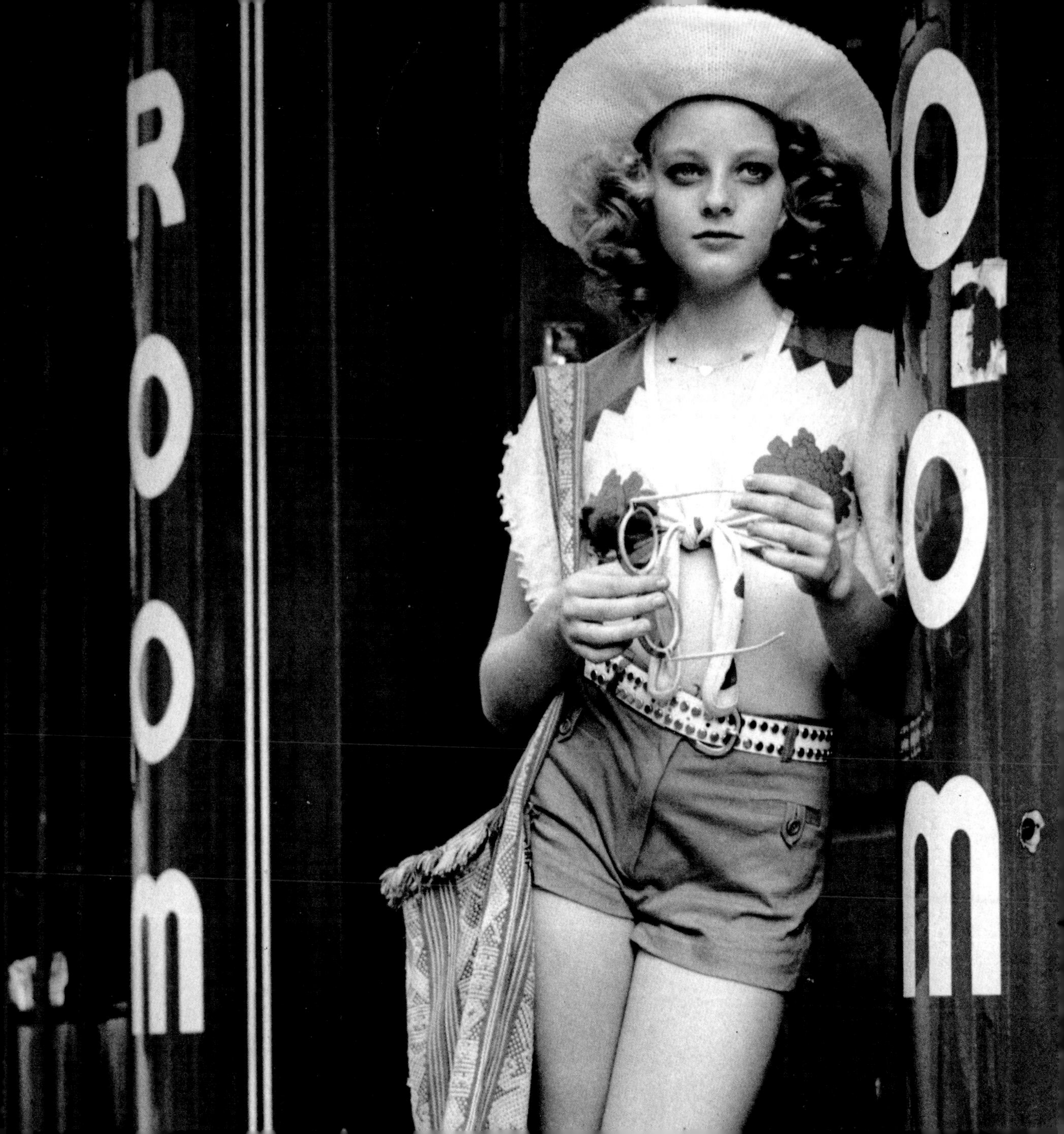
ROOM

Brooke Shields

PRETTY BABY, 1978 (ABOVE)

*A child actress with an unsettling adult-like beauty, the one-time baby model
and daughter of professional stage mom Terri Shields made a controversial starring debut
playing a child prostitute in this rather tame (by today's standards) Louis Malle-directed
story set in a 1917 New Orleans brothel. Despite cries of child abuse and kiddie pornography
(Shields wore a body stocking to simulate a few nude scenes), the picture remains the best
work of the sometime-actress and Princeton graduate, whose equally controversial Calvin
Klein ad campaigns ("Nothing comes between me and my Calvins") sustained Shields's
celebrity more than any of her lackluster follow-up efforts in films such as*
The Blue Lagoon, Endless Love, *and* Backstreet Dreams.

Mariel Hemingway

LIPSTICK, 1976 (RIGHT)

*Any movie promoted with the line "Rape was only the beginning!" was bound to cause
some controversy, especially when it featured Ernest Hemingway's underage (14) grand-
daughter in a number of exploitative situations. Starring supermodel Margaux Hemingway
as the ultimate "fashion victim," the tawdry tale of a model who is molested by a composer
marked the film debut of younger sister Mariel, who, after an Oscar-nominated star turn in*
Manhattan, *aroused even more controversy as an Olympic athlete who goes after a gold medal
(and the love of a female competitor!) in the titillating but tasteless* Personal Best.

Aileen Quinn, center

ANNIE, 1982

*Even the appealing antics of carrot-topped Quinn (and a stellar
cast led by Albert Finney, Carol Burnett, and Bernadette Peters) couldn't
save this curiously stagebound film adaptation of the hit Broadway
musical based on the "Little Orphan Annie" comic strip from box-office
disaster. Produced to the staggering tune of over $40 million, the highly
publicized venture was memorialized by* Time *magazine with the line,
"Funeral services may be held starting this week at a theater near
you," and marked the first and last attempt by Oscar-winner
John Huston to direct a musical.*

Kelly Reno (with Black)

THE BLACK STALLION, 1979

*Although Reno shines in this exquisitely photographed
modern-day classic based on the popular children's novel by Walter
Farley, it was the long-ago costar of* National Velvet, *Mickey Rooney,
who was deservedly nominated for a Best Supporting Actor Oscar for his
role as the trainer who leads the stallion to victory. Followed four years
later by* The Black Stallion Returns *(with Reno now a teen-aged
jockey), the sentimental but well-made adventure flick appealed
as much to adults as it did to children.*

Henry Thomas

E.T. THE EXTRA-TERRESTRIAL, 1982

*The sci-fi classic that became a part of American popular culture
as soon as it was released also introduced two of the most promising
child actors of the 1980s. Although Thomas has worked steadily throughout the past decade, it is movie-kid-sister Drew Barrymore, scion of the
celebrated acting clan, who has continuously courted the limelight in
her transformation from child star and real-life troubled teen to
grown-up actress and media celebrity.*

Ricky Schroder (with Jon Voight)
THE CHAMP, 1979 (ABOVE)

A remake of the tearful 1931 Jackie Cooper/Wallace Beery hit about an adoring son who is his washed-up-prizefighter dad's only fan, the soft-focus Franco Zeffirelli update displayed the lachrymose talents of its eight-year-old star for the first time. Set at the Hialeah Racetrack in Florida and costarring Faye Dunaway as the child's equally weepy mom, the film paved the way for Schroder's future success in films and his starring role in the long-running hit television series "Silver Spoons."

Lukas Haas (with Harrison Ford)
WITNESS, 1985 (RIGHT)

Produced at the relatively low cost of $12 million, this eight-times-nominated Oscar winner more than returned its investment and made a star of eight-year-old Haas in the process. The story of an Amish boy who unwittingly witnesses a drug-related big-city murder, the beautifully photographed thriller-cum-love story was only the second screen appearance for its young costar, who has since gone on to make a number of films as a promising actor in teenage roles.

Macaulay Culkin (with Joe Pesci and Daniel Stern)
HOME ALONE 2: LOST IN NEW YORK, 1992 (ABOVE)

*Reprising the part that had made him an instant celebrity two years earlier,
Culkin became the richest youngster in Hollywood history when he was reportedly
paid $5 million and 5 percent of the gross for this Big Apple Christmastime sequel.
More violent and not as funny as the first film, the second nevertheless packed in
audiences who couldn't get enough of the mischievous movie mogul in his
slapstick quest to thwart the stupidest stooges since Moe, Larry, and Curly.*

Macaulay Culkin
HOME ALONE, 1990 (RIGHT)

*Although the nine-year-old's classic shaving scene isn't as funny the third time
around, John Hughes's surprise holiday smash hit became the biggest-grossing film
of 1990 and the most lucrative comedy of all time. It also made an overnight sensation of actress Bonnie Bedelia's pint-size nephew, whose sadistic celluloid antics had
audiences doubled over with laughter and the Hollywood powers-that-be scrambling
to cash in on the film industry's hottest juvenile property in recent memory.*

Macaulay Culkin and Anna Chlumsky
MY GIRL, 1991 (RIGHT)
Promoted with the shameless line, "Mac's back and he's not alone,"
this touching film about an eleven-year-old girl's coming to terms with
life, love, and puberty marked the auspicious debut for Culkin's precocious
costar. Fans of the wildly popular ten-year-old actor turned out in droves
to see the star of Home Alone *get his first screen kiss, making this*
Columbia Pictures release another box-office bonanza for
Hollywood's boy-wonder money-making machine.

Jason James Richter (with Keiko)
FREE WILLY, 1993 (FOLLOWING PAGES)
Take an appealing young boy, a friendly killer whale named Willy,
and a soundtrack by megastar Michael Jackson, and what do you get?
A box-office smash for the whole family. The most recent entry in a long
line of boy-and-animal Hollywood crowd-pleasers, this sappy story of a
youngster who schemes to free an amusement-park whale introduced
Richter as the big screen's pre-adolescent flavor of the moment and
made a real star of an underwater giant named Keiko.

Christina Ricci
THE ADDAMS FAMILY, 1991

*As wee-little she-devil Wednesday Addams, Ricci held her own
against the considerable talents of Raul Julia and Anjelica Huston in
this feature-film composite of Charles Addams's original* New Yorker
*cartoons and the popular 1960s television series by the same name.
Reprising her debut role two years later for the vastly superior* Addams
Family Values, *the precocious newcomer was even more morbidly
fascinating as the petite, post-Gothic punk who takes on a campful
of picture-perfect all-American kids and sends them packing.*

PROJECT EDITOR: J. C. SUARÈS
TEXT: J. SPENCER BECK
PICTURE EDITOR: LESLIE FRATKIN